WILLIAM SHAKESPEARE'S
THE
TEMPEST

RETOLD BY
BRUCE COVILLE

ILLUSTRATED BY
RUTH SANDERSON

A PICTURE YEARLING BOOK

Published by
Bantam Doubleday Dell Books for Young Readers
a division of
Bantam Doubleday Dell Publishing Group, Inc.
1540 Broadway
New York, New York 10036

ISBN: 0-440-41297-8

Reprinted by arrangement with Doubleday Books for Young Readers
Printed in the United States of America

October 1996
10 9 8 7 6 5 4 3 2 1
DAN

"We are such stuff as dreams are made on..."

Act IV, Scene 1

ONCE ON A TIME A MAGICIAN named Prospero served as duke in the city of Milan. Prospero loved his books, and spent so many hours poring over dusty volumes of strange lore that he left the day-to-day business of running the city to his brother Antonio.

In time, Antonio began to feel that the dukedom should be his in truth. So he contacted Prospero's enemy, the king of Naples, and the two secretly plotted against Prospero.

One dark night soon after, Antonio opened the city gates to the king and his forces. Prospero and his tiny child, Miranda, were stolen from the palace and set adrift in a boat so leaky and rotten that even the rats had abandoned it.

They had one piece of good fortune: the man assigned to prepare the boat was secretly a friend of Prospero's and had managed to sneak on board not only food and water but fine clothing and Prospero's great book of spells.

As they drifted through hot days and dark nights, only Miranda's cheerful smiles kept the magician from despair. Finally one evening the wind blew the voyagers to the shore of a strange, spirit-haunted island.

Prospero made a fire on the beach and prepared a place for them to rest. But as darkness fell, the night was disturbed by weird and mournful cries drifting from the forest.

STRAPPING MIRANDA TO HIS back, Prospero went in search of the sorrow. Deep in the woods he found a pine tree that had been split by lightning many years before. The cries seemed to issue from the tree itself. Prospero studied the charred, split trunk, then lifted his staff and spoke words of power. At once a spirit of the air burst forth.

"Speak, spirit," commanded Prospero. "Tell me your name and how you came to be entrapped here."

"I am Ariel," breathed the spirit, stretching and dancing in the air. "And I was bound in that woody cell by a witch named Sycorax when I refused to do her evil work. She died soon after, leaving me trapped here for twelve long years."

"Then in exchange for my releasing you, for twelve years shall you serve me," said Prospero. "However, you will find that I ask no ill of you."

Glad to be free of the pine, Ariel agreed to Prospero's demand. But no sooner had the pact been pledged than a hairy, misshapen monster came roaring out of the darkness.

"STAY, BEAST!" CRIED PROSPERO, pointing his staff at the monster. The creature stopped in midcharge, frozen in a beam of moonlight. Prospero circled it, staring at its hideous form.

"Ariel, what know you of this sad creature?"

"'Tis the child of that same Sycorax," whispered Ariel. "She served a demon lord named Setebos. When her ways proved too wicked for the people of her city, they drove her out. She fled to this island, where she gave birth to the thing you see before you. His name is Caliban, and if you would heed my warning, then cast him into the sea and be done with him."

But Prospero, himself an exile, would not allow such a thing. "Let us try to tame this savage creature," he said.

Thus the magician and his daughter, the airy spirit and the wretched monster formed a household on the haunted island. With Caliban's help, Prospero found a large, dry cave that had many chambers. Using his magic arts, the magician transformed the cave into a home both cozy and secure. There he settled to raise his daughter and study his books.

At first Prospero treated Caliban as tenderly as his own child. The monster, grateful for such attention, showed the mage where to find good fruit and sweet water.

Miranda, too, was kind to Caliban. As she grew older, she spent many hours teaching him to speak. And for a time the monster appeared truly changed.

But this did not last, for Caliban's heart was twisted beyond all repair. In time, he grew jealous of Prospero's love for Miranda. When his jealousy grew so great that he tried to harm the child, he was banished from the cave and given only lowly tasks.

Thereafter Caliban nursed a hatred for the magician that grew deeper and darker by the day. And Miranda, who had once befriended the monster, feared to be near him.

Yet for the most part the child's life was sweet. With Ariel protecting her, she grew wild and free, roaming the island's beaches, climbing its rocky shores, and scrambling through its tangled forests. At night her father taught her from his books, telling her stories both strange and wonderful.

Despite all this, she longed for company her own age.

AS FOR PROSPERO, HE CONTINUED to study his magic, growing ever wiser and more powerful. Yet just as the island was haunted by spirits, so Prospero was haunted by the memory of his traitorous brother and the dukedom that was rightfully his.

His day of vengeance came during their twelfth year on the island. Miranda was then fourteen years old, and her beauty was like that of a rose just beginning to open. One afternoon she was dancing on the beach when she saw a strange shape gliding across the waters. After a moment she realized that it was a ship.

Climbing a low cliff, Miranda lay on her stomach to watch the vessel's progress. "Come to our shore," she whispered longingly. But to her sorrow it seemed that the ship would pass the island altogether.

Just as she gave up hope of a closer look at the ship and its passengers, a great tempest arose. Jagged streaks of lightning sizzled through the sky. Waves as high as the cliff from which she watched tossed the ship from side to side. She could hear the cries of the terrified men on board even above the howling wind.

Then Miranda heard another cry, wild and fierce, but close at hand.

T

URNING, SHE SAW HER FATHER
on the rocks above her, staff upraised, eyes wild.

"Father!" she cried, scrambling up the rocks to throw herself
at his feet. "Father! If by your art you have put the wild waters
in this roar, then I cry mercy! My heart aches for the poor souls
on that ship."

Prospero ignored her, his attention all on his magic.

"Father!" cried Miranda. "Harm them not!"

Still the magician ignored his daughter as he swung his staff
through the air, directing the winds that buffeted the ship.

"Father!" cried Miranda a third time. "Spare them!"

"Be done!" roared the magician.

At once a calm fell on the ocean. Miranda turned her eyes
from her father to see if the ship was safe.

To her astonishment, it had vanished.

"Be not alarmed," said Prospero gently. "I swear to you that not one of the men on that ship has come to harm."

"But why have you done such a thing?" asked Miranda.

Prospero hesitated. Then, with a sigh, he told her for the first time the sad history of their betrayal and exile.

"What has this to do with the ship?" asked Miranda.

"It has all to do. For by my art I know who rides that vessel — the brother who betrayed me, and the king who helped him do it. This is the day when I must seize my fate or remain island-bound forever. And so, sweet Miranda — sleep for a bit."

Then with a gentle spell he closed his daughter's eyes, so he could consult with Ariel, which he ever did in private. "To me, my spirit," he whispered. "To me, to tell me all!"

Swift as thought, Ariel rode the wind to Prospero's side. "Oh, master, well have I worked your wishes. I flamed wonder all about the ship, until astonishment overwhelmed 'em. Some leapt into the raging sea. Others hid below the decks. Yet all, my lord, are safe as you commanded."

"And the ship?" asked Prospero.

"Harbored on the island's far side, safe and dry, its crew caught in mystic slumber. As for the passengers, they are spread across the island's shore, the king set far from his son so that each mourns bitterly, thinking the other dead."

"Well done, my heart!" cried Prospero. "But serve me out this day and you shall be as free as mountain winds. Now, go you all invisible and fetch that king's son to my cave, where Miranda and I will meet you anon."

ARIEL RODE THE WIND TO THE beach, where the prince, Ferdinand by name, sat weeping for his lost father. Circling above him, the spirit began to play a sad, haunting song.

Ferdinand jumped to his feet. "Where can this music be coming from?" he cried.

Ariel did not answer, only continued to play. Lured by the strange melody, Ferdinand pursued the invisible spirit through the haunted woods until, mystified and mourning, he came to Prospero's cave. In front of the cave sat Miranda, combing her hair.

Deep as was the prince's grief for his father, deeper still was his astonishment at seeing Miranda. "Are you the goddess who sent this strange music?" he whispered.

"I am but a maid, good sir," replied Miranda, delighted at this wonderful young man, so unlike either her father or Caliban.

Prospero, who was watching from the cave, was delighted as well, for it was his plan that the two should fall in love. But he soon grew troubled. Though Miranda and Ferdinand appeared to be falling in love, they were doing so far too quickly for his taste.

"**S**O SWIFT A LOVE WILL NEVER last," Prospero muttered to himself. "It must face some obstacle to give it strength." Knowing this, he stepped from the cave and roared, "Who are you that dare disturb my daughter?"

"Father," cried Miranda, "why so angry?"

"Silence, child! I ask again, sir: Who are you?"

"I am, alas, the king of Naples," said Ferdinand sadly.

Prospero laughed. "A king? You are barely a man!"

"The king, my father, was lost in the tempest," said Ferdinand. "By that loss I gained the crown—which I would gladly exchange for my father's life."

Though this answer pleased Prospero, he was not yet ready to put Ferdinand at ease. "I say you are a fraud, come to steal my island and my daughter. Now you shall be my servant instead."

"The king of Naples serves no man!" cried Ferdinand, drawing his sword.

Prospero had but to move a finger and Ferdinand's sword grew so heavy the prince could not hold it up. Then the magician showed him a great pile of muddy logs and commanded him to carry them to the cave. And all this he did so that Ferdinand would not think Miranda too easily won.

ONCE FERDINAND WAS AT
work, Prospero called Ariel and said, "Now lead me to my
enemies." Traveling invisibly, magician and spirit found the
king and his men searching the beach for any sign of Ferdinand.
The king, sure that his son was drowned, wept and moaned.

When Prospero heard some of the men complain of great
hunger, he called the spirits of the island to bring forth a banquet
table piled high with tempting foods. As the aromas of warm
bread and spicy meat filled the air, one of the men whispered,
"Now I will believe that there are unicorns!"

Dancing graciously, the spirits invited the men to eat. But
before they could touch their first bite, Ariel swooped to the
table in the guise of a harpy. The men drew back in fear. The
harpy clapped its brazen wings, and the food vanished in a blaze
of light.

"Oh, you men of sin!" roared Ariel, pointing first to the
king, then to Prospero's brother. "Remember now your crimes
against Prospero, the duke of Milan, and his infant daughter,
Miranda. Remember, and repent of your wickedness!"

Astonished that this creature knew their past, the king and
Antonio fell to the ground, weeping with guilt and fear.

Prospero was well pleased. When Ariel returned to his side,
he whispered, "Now fly you and see what Caliban does, while
I look in on Miranda and Ferdinand."

ARIEL FOUND CALIBAN TRUDGING along the beach with a load of wood. Suddenly the monster stopped. Ahead was an oddly dressed man. Fearing it was a spirit sent to torment him for dawdling, the beast fell to the ground and tried to hide beneath his tattered coat.

But the man was only the king's jester, Trinculo. None too bright to begin with, he was now quite addled with his near escape from drowning. Stumbling over Caliban, he cried, "Is this a man or a fish? Phew! A fish by the smell of it!"

A rumble of thunder shook the dark sky. "Another storm!" cried Trinculo. "If it is like the last, I shall be drowned as I stand!" And with that he crawled under Caliban's cloak to shelter himself.

"They make a rare pair," chuckled Ariel.

Soon the king's butler, Stephano, came along. He had floated to shore on a barrel of wine washed overboard from the ship. In his relief at surviving, he had proceeded to drink far more of the wine than was wise. Now, stumbling over Caliban and Trinculo, the drunken butler decided he had found a two-headed monster. "I fear you not, you mooncalf!" he roared, brandishing a wine container he had made from tree bark.

"Oh, spirit, do not torment me!" pleaded Caliban. "I swear I'll bring the wood home faster!"

"It speaks my language!" cried Stephano in astonishment.

"Is that you, Stephano?" asked Trinculo.

Soon monster, jester, and butler had untangled themselves from Caliban's cloak. Then Stephano passed around his wine.

Caliban thought the wine quite wonderful and began to look on Stephano with admiration. With a bit more wine he decided that anyone who offered such a drink must be a god.

"I shall be your servant!" he cried, covering Stephano's feet with kisses. "I will even show you the fiend who stole this island from me. I know when he naps. You can kill him then and take both the island and his daughter for yourself."

When Stephano agreed, Caliban leapt for joy, singing:

"'Ban, 'Ban, Ca — Caliban
Has a new master. Get a new man!"

But when he set out to lead Stephano and Trinculo to the magician's cave, Ariel lured them into a sticky bog to delay them. Then the faithful spirit flew to Prospero to warn him of the danger.

Meanwhile, Ferdinand was hard at the labors Prospero had set for him. Miranda wept to see him working so. "Allow me to do it for you!" she cried, reaching for the logs.

"Nonsense, fair one," said Ferdinand. "With your face before me the work is light."

Prospero had been looking on in secret for some time. As he watched Ferdinand toil at his lowly task without complaint, he was convinced that the prince's love was true.

Prospero went to his daughter. "Come, my child," he said gently. Leading her to Ferdinand's side, he joined their hands.

"All these vexations were but my trials of your love," he said to the prince. "Well have you stood the test. Now do I bless your betrothal." Then he called the spirits of the island to appear as goddesses and bless the forthcoming marriage.

But the celebration had hardly begun when Ariel arrived to tell his master of Caliban's dark plan.

"Alas, our revels now are ended," said Prospero, and with a wave of his staff he caused the spirits to melt back into the air. Then, after commanding the puzzled lovers to take shelter in the cave, he strode off to deal with Caliban.

ARIEL FLEW AT PROSPERO'S SIDE.

"The traitor is slogging through the bog into which I lured him. But it will not be long before he breaks free and leads the men to your home."

Prospero soon thought of a plan. "Go and bring me the finest of my clothing," he said to Ariel.

Ariel did as Prospero asked. Then the two of them went to a clearing through which they knew Caliban must pass, and hung the clothing upon the trees surrounding it.

Before long, Caliban, Trinculo, and Stephano arrived. Hiding outside the clearing, magician and spirit watched as the men halted, enchanted by the clothes.

"Don't stop now!" pleaded Caliban. "First kill Prospero! Then clothes, daughter, and island will all be yours."

His pleas were to no avail. Stephano and Trinculo, never having seen such finery, longed to try it on. As they gave their attention to the clothing, Prospero commanded the spirits of the island to appear as ferocious hounds. Eyes glowing, teeth bared, they bounded into the clearing.

Shrieking with terror, the plotters went bounding out.

"Now does my project gather to a head," said Prospero. "Fly, Ariel, and lead the king and his men to my cave."

NOT LONG AFTER, THE MAGE stood in his cave, preparing for his final revenge. But as he put on his great cloak, Ariel returned. "Oh, master," said the spirit, "could you but see the king and your once-traitorous brother weeping for their wrongs, it would prick your heart to pity. A rock would crack, a tree bleed sap in sorrow at their sorrow."

Prospero was touched by Ariel's words. "If you, who are but air, can feel such tenderness toward these men, should not I, a man, find it in me to forgive?"

He sat and bowed his head in thought. For a long time he was silent, for it was not easy to give up his anger. "Ariel," he said at last, "bring them to me. When all is done, I shall destroy my staff and in the ocean drown my book and, setting aside this rough magic, free you and all the spirits of this island."

Within moments the king and his men stood before Prospero's cave. What astonishment there was among them to see the rightful duke alive — and what fear, as they thought again of how they had wronged him. But as they wept and begged forgiveness, Prospero smiled. "I grant you life," he said, "and with it the chance to remedy the wrong you have done me."

When the king and Antonio renounced all claim to Milan, Prospero said to the king, "Now in return I shall bring forth a wonder to content you as much as my dukedom does me."

Then he drew aside the curtain that covered his cave. Behind it sat Miranda and Ferdinand, playing at a game of chess.

Miranda, who had never seen so many people together, reached for Ferdinand's hand. "How many goodly creatures are there here!" she whispered. "O brave new world, that has such people in it!"

The king wept with joy to see his son alive again.

"I have cursed the sea without cause," said Ferdinand, as he went to embrace his father.

Ariel added to the delight by bringing forth the king's ship from the cavern where it had been hidden.

Finally, at Prospero's behest, the spirit drove Trinculo, Stephano, and Caliban in from the forest. "These two men, I think, are yours," said Prospero. "But this thing of darkness, I acknowledge mine."

"I'll be wise hereafter, and seek for grace," said Caliban. "What a thrice-double ass was I, to take this drunkard for a god."

THAT NIGHT PROSPERO CLIMBED alone to the highest point of the island. Raising his staff, he hurled it to the winds. Next he flung aside his book, crying "Now my charms are all o'erthrown, and what strength I have's mine own."

Ariel caught the magical items and carried them far beneath the waters to a place both deep and safe, where they would lie forever.

Then Prospero bid freedom and farewell to Ariel, whom, in truth, he loved nearly as much as he loved Miranda.

At dawn the faithful spirit freely provided a final gift: fair winds to carry the rightful duke, the young lovers, and all other human souls from the enchanted island back to Naples, where Ferdinand and Miranda would soon be wed.

AUTHOR'S NOTE

The Tempest is a gorgeous fairy tale of a play, and a perfect introduction to Shakespeare for younger readers. It is also a play that young people *should* know. Prospero, Miranda, Ariel, and Caliban have entered the culture as icons, and to be unaware of their provenance means missing references that are sometimes simply fun, sometimes a vital clue to what an author or artist is trying to do. In short, knowing these characters is a perfect example of what has come to be called "cultural literacy."

These characters and their interplay are the foremost glory of *The Tempest*, and as I worked on this adaptation, I came to understand why so many other writers have felt an urge to bring them to life in new ways. However, my mission here is not to invent a new story, but to present an accurate, easily accessible version of the story Shakespeare created nearly four hundred years ago.

I have varied from the play in two major ways: Shakespeare told his story in a single day, which put a number of constraints on the action, and required his characters to do a lot of explaining. For the sake of clarity, I untangled the threads of the story and started at the beginning. The second change was the elimination of a subplot regarding an attempt on King Alonso's life.

Finally, this book is not meant as a substitute for, but as an invitation to, the splendors that await in not only *The Tempest*, but all of Shakespeare's works. Our hope is that it will inspire young people to experience the play itself—and in the process discover that Shakespeare is more fun and less intimidating than they may have believed.

—*Bruce Coville*